DON'T TOSS GRAN
IN THE BEGONIA

C000059280

Faut pas pousser mémé dans les bégonias

Proverbes et dictons français
Marie-Hélène Claudel-Gilly

English proverbs and sayings
Primrose Arnander

Illustrations Kathryn Lamb
Introduction Michael Edwards

Also available in this series:

You Can't Get Blood out of a Turnip (Italian)
Apricots Tomorrow (Arabic)
The Son of a Duck is a Floater (Arabic)
Pavilions in the Air (Chinese)
Unload Your Own Donkey (Arabic)

DON'T TOSS GRANNY IN THE BEGONIAS

Medina Publishing Ltd
310 Ewell Road
Surbiton, Surrey KT6 7AL
Tel: +44 (0)20 8399 7736
www.medinapublishing.com

Reprinted 2017

ISBN 978-1-911487-01-2

British Library Cataloguing-in-Publication Data
A catalogue record for this publication is available from the British Library

Printed and bound by Short Run Press Ltd, UK

Medina Publishing

INTRODUCTION

The pleasing thing about proverbs is that they make us feel intelligent. All that practical wisdom in so few words! *Don't put the cart before the horse, L'habit ne fait pas le moine* ... Very often snappily expressed – *Birds of a feather flock together, Qui va à la chasse perd sa place* – they grant us the gift of eloquence. Their unexpected images appeal to our fantasy: *If wishes were horses, beggars would ride, Tomber comme un cheveu sur la soupe*, while their comic sharpness: *Youth is wasted on the young, Plus ça change, plus c'est la même chose*, awakens our wit. And if we stare long enough at those familiar sayings, they can seem to slide and merge, to produce, for example, the perfectly plausible *One swallow does not make a meal* or rather surrealist *Let sleeping logs die*.

Between English and French proverbs one might have looked for large differences. How can our two peoples say similar things, and so come to understand each other, when the French believe that the English go in for a healthy exercise called footing, and the English imagine the French tripping the light fantastic in a *palais de danse*? National characteristics do sometimes show through. One glimpses the longer survival in France of traditional farming in *Il ne faut pas mettre la charrue avant les boeufs*, and the eternal tribulations of the English in *It never rains but it pours*. English proverbs are also, generally speaking, more compact: *Easy come, easy go, Once bitten, twice shy, More haste less speed*. They benefit from the directness and concision which have helped to promote English as the world language. This does not necessarily make them superior. The recorded voice in the London Underground warns passengers at certain stations to *Mind the gap* (with a 1940s upper crust accent – ma(h)-eend the gep – which can startle). The version in the Paris metro seems, by comparison, long-winded: *Attention à la marche en descendant du train*, but turns out to be an elegant line of verse, an alexandrine.

Yet the French in their proverbs are quite as hard-headed, and quite as interested in the realities of the social and of the natural worlds, as are the English, and not at all rationalist and idealizing. The two countries come together in their proverbs, on the level of how to get by in a rough world. As perhaps do most countries, in which case international meetings ought to begin with an exchange, not of compliments, but of proverbs. This book performs that exchange, and shows that, despite their inveterate wariness, the French and English join hands in coping wryly with things as they are. By its comic take on so many situations it draws everyone even closer in laughter. The English and French are an odd couple who, from time immemorial, like to dislike – or is it dislike liking? – each other. Fortunately, old enemies make the best friends.

Michael Edwards
Professor
Collège de France, Paris

AUTHORS' PREFACE

*D*on't Toss Granny in the Begonias is the sixth in a series of illustrated bilingual proverb books. Their origins go back 25 years to a meeting between Primrose and the late Ashkhain Skipwith with their Yemeni hostess in Sana'a, who suddenly quoted the picturesque Arabic proverb *Money delivers the genie bound.* Flights of fancy rose from that image, which was so unlike pipers being commanded to play a chosen tune and from them emerged *The Son of a Duck is a Floater* and two successor volumes of Arabic proverbs, to be joined by similar books of Italian and Chinese proverbs. Kathryn Lamb has memorably illustrated them all.

Some of our French proverbs are not in the established canon. Marie-Hélène's grandfather, the poet-diplomat Paul Claudel used to say *La mort est un examen difficile à passer, mais il y a un avantage . . . tout le monde est reçu.* Primrose's father was head of a female household; did he invent *Trois filles et la mère font le diable pour le père* or was he told it by a sympathetic friend during one of the many Anglo-French transport conferences which he attended?

This book follows the formula of its predecessors. Each French proverb is given a literal translation and an English equivalent, with interspersed cartoons. The proverbs are sometimes identical; they can also be startingly different, as our title illustrates. We sometimes add a quotation to show the usage or meaning. In some cases, we add a slang equivalent, 'proverbs in waiting' one might call them; for example, the American saying *If it ain't broke don't fix it* is similar to *On ne change pas une équipe qui gagne*. Many proverbs are known in abbreviated form; we normally say *Talk of the devil* without adding *and he is sure to appear*. Some French proverbs and sayings are used untranslated in English, such as *Noblesse oblige*.

Don't Toss Granny in the Begonias is not intended to be a major work of scholarship, but rather to provide light entertainment. We have found that, as ever, there is much disagreement amongst French and English speakers about the precise meaning of some proverbs; we fully expect to be challenged on their *nuances*. We hope that the assemblage of comparative proverbs and sayings will give as much pleasure to our readers as its preparation has to us.

Primrose Arnander
London

Marie-Hélène Claudel-Gilly
Paris

Comme un éléphant dans un magasin de porcelaine

Like an elephant in a porcelain shop

Like a bull in a china shop

Se mettre sur son 31

To put oneself in 31 mode

To be dressed to the nines

La nuit porte conseil

The night brings advice

Night is the mother of counsel

Chaque renard porte sa queue à sa manière

Each fox carries his own tail in his own way

Every man after his fashion

9

Faire d'un œuf un bœuf

To make an ox out of an egg

To make a mountain out of a molehill

On ne peut pas sonner la cloche et suivre la procession

One cannot ring the bell and follow the procession

You cannot run with the hare and hunt with the hounds

Quand les poules auront des dents

When hens will have teeth

When pigs fly

American *When hell freezes over*

11

Etre assis entre deux chaises

To sit between two chairs

To sit on the fence

Mettre la puce à l'oreille de quelqu'un

To put a flea on someone's ear

To start a hare [start an uncomfortable train of thought]

[In English to *give someone a flea in his ear* is to scold that person roundly]

Il est haut comme trois pommes

He is as tall as three apples

He is knee high to a grasshopper

Aide-toi le ciel t'aidera

Aid yourself, heaven will aid you

God helps those who help themselves

Les vieilles poules font le meilleur bouillon

The old hens make the best soup

The best wine comes out of an old bottle

Mêle-toi de tes oignons

Look after your own onions

Mind your own business

Un chien regarde bien un évêque

A dog may well look at a bishop

A cat may look at a king

Il n'est pas dans son assiette

He is not in his plate

He is out of sorts

Loin des yeux, loin du cœur

Far from the eyes, far from the heart

Out of sight out of mind

Pratiquer la politique de l'autruche

To follow the strategy of the ostrich

To bury your head in the sand

Chassez le naturel, il revient au galop

Chase off what is natural and it comes galloping back

A leopard cannot change his spots

Argent mal acquis ne profite jamais

Ill gained money never brings profit

Ill gotten gains never prosper

Plautus, Paenulus *Male partum male disperit*

Au premier son on ne prend pas la caille

One cannot capture the quail on the first call

Softly, softly catchee monkey

Saisir la balle au bond

To seize the ball on the bounce

Strike while the iron is hot

La chance sourit aux audacieux

Fortune smiles at the bold

Fortune favours the bold

Virgil, Aeneid *Audentis fortuna juvat*

Quand les brebis enragent elles sont pires que les loups

When the ewes are angry they are worse than wolves

Even a worm will turn

William Congreve *Hell hath no fury like woman scorned*

L'habit ne fait pas le moine

The habit does not make the monk

You cannot tell a book by its cover

Arabic proverb *Not everything with a crooked neck is a camel*

Cœur facile à donner facile à ôter

Heart easily given is easily taken back

Easy come, easy go

Pour l'amour du chevalier la dame aime l'écuyer

For the love of the knight, the lady woos the squire

To set a sprat to catch a mackerel

Un bon tiens vaut mieux que deux tu l'auras

One grasp now is better than two in future

A bird in the hand is worth two in the bush

Science sans conscience n'est que ruine de l'âme

Science without conscience ruins the soul

Theodore Roosevelt *To educate a man in mind and not in morals*
is to educate a menace to society

Ce n'est pas au vieux singe qu'on apprend à faire des grimaces

You don't teach an old monkey to pull faces

You can't teach an old dog new tricks

Il n'est point de bonheur sans nuage

There is no happiness without clouds

There is no pleasure without pain

Qui va à la chasse perd sa place

Who goes hunting loses his position

Finders keepers, losers weepers

Spanish proverb *The one who went to Seville lost his seat*

Les chiens ne font pas des chats

Dogs do not give birth to cats

Like breeds like

Celui qui se noie ne regarde pas l'eau qu'il boit

A man who is drowning does not consider the water he is drinking

A drowning man will clutch at any straw

C'est donnant, donnant

It is giving, giving

You scratch my back and I'll scratch yours

American *There's no such thing as a free lunch*

Marcher sur des œufs

To walk on eggs

Treading on eggshells

Il a mangé de la vache enragée

He has eaten the meat of a mad cow

He is on his uppers

Un homme sans argent est un loup sans dents

A man without money is like a wolf without teeth

Money makes a man

Sydney Smith *Poverty is no disgrace to a man, but it is counfoundedly inconvenient*

Il a vendu son cochon

He has sold his pig

He has burnt his boats

Harold Macmillan called it *selling the family silver*

On sait ce que l'on quitte on ne sait pas ce que l'on prend

One knows what one leaves, not what one gets

Better the devil you know [than the devil you don't know]

Shakespeare, Hamlet

. . . the dread of something after death
. . . makes us rather bear those ills we have . . .
Than fly to others that we know not of?

Autant de têtes, autant d'avis

As many heads as opinions

Too many cooks spoil the broth

On est tous dans le même bain

We're all in the same bath

We're all in the same boat

Il ne faut pas pousser mémé dans les bégonias

Don't toss granny in the begonias

Don't overegg the pudding

Quand on veut, on peut

When one wants, one can

Where there's a will, there's a way

Nous avons tous assez de force pour supporter les maux des autres

We all have enough strength to bear the misfortunes of others

It is easy to bear the misfortune of others

Oliver Goldsmith *Ay, people are generally calm at the misfortune of others*

Il faut hurler avec les loups

One must howl with the wolves

When in Rome, do as the Romans do

Ne comptez pas les œufs dans le derrière d'une poule

Don't count the eggs in a chicken's backside

Don't count your chickens before they hatch

Avoir l'esprit d'escalier

[*French proverb often used untranslated*]

To have the wit of the staircase

It is easy to be wise after the event

[Alternative interpretation *Below stairs tittle-tattle*]

Renard qui dort la matinée n'a pas la langue emplumée

The fox that sleeps in the early morning does not have a tongue covered in feathers

The early bird catches the worm

In ne faut pas mettre la charrue avant les bœufs

One must not put the plough in front of the oxen

Don't put the cart before the horse

Au plus débile la chandelle à la main

To the weakest the candle is given to hold

The weakest go to the wall

American *Never give a sucker an even break*

Elle fait la sainte-nitouche

She plays the part of saint 'no touch'

Butter wouldn't melt in her mouth

Like the 18th century fictional character *Little Goody Two-shoes*

Les belles plumes font les beaux oiseaux

Fine feathers make fine birds

Quand le vin est tiré il faut le boire

When the cork is drawn, you must drink the wine

In for a penny, in for a pound

Un malheur ne vient jamais seul

A misfortune never comes alone

It never rains but it pours

Shakespeare, Hamlet *When sorrows come, they come not single spies, but in battalions*

Tomber comme un cheveu sur la soupe

To turn up like a hair in the soup

A blot on the landscape

S'entendre comme des larrons en foire

To understand one another like thieves in the market

To be as thick as thieves

Chien qui aboie ne mord pas

The dog that barks does not bite

His bark is worse than his bite

Il a avalé son parapluie

He has swallowed his umbrella

He is uptight

In *GoldenEye* Jack Wade calls James Bond *another stiff-ass Brit, with your secret codes and your passwords*

Du dit au fait, il y a un grand trait

From speech to action is a long gap

Fine words butter no parsnips

American *All hat and no cattle*

Trop parler nuit, trop gratter cuit

Too much talking harms, too much scratching burns

Least said soonest mended

La nuit tous les chats sont gris

At night all the cats are grey

All cats are grey in the dark

Faute de grives, on mange des merles

In the absence of thrushes, one eats blackbirds

Beggars can't be choosers

Arabic proverb *For want of a donkey, they saddle the dogs*

Il se croit le premier moutardier du Pape

He thinks he's the pope's top mustard maker

He thinks he's the bee's knees

The French Pope John XXII (1316-1334), who was very keen on mustard,
is supposed to have made his nephew *premier moutardier du Pape*

La moutarde lui est montée au nez

The mustard went up his nose

He blew his top

Porter l'eau à la rivière

To carry water to the river

To carry coals to Newcastle

On ne prend pas les mouches avec du vinaigre

One cannot catch flies with vinegar

Honey catches more flies than vinegar

Etre à cheval sur les règles

To be riding on top of the rules

To be a stickler for the rules

Il prend une massue pour tuer une mouche

He takes a club to kill a fly

To use a sledgehammer to crack a nut

Avec des si et des mais, on mettrait Paris en bouteille

With ifs and buts, one could put Paris in a bottle

If wishes were horses, beggars would ride

Charles Kingsley, Alton Locke
If ifs and ans were pots and pans,
There'd be no work for tinkers' hands.

Plus ça change, plus c'est la même chose
[*The French proverb is often used untranslated*]

The more it changes, the more it stays the same

There is nothing new under the sun

Quand on parle du loup on en voit la queue

When one mentions the wolf, one sees his tail

Talk of the devil [and he's sure to appear]

Qui s'y frotte s'y pique

Who rubs against it is stung by it

If you play with fire, you will get burnt

Qui s'excuse, s'accuse

He who excuses himself accuses himself

Shakespeare, King John
And oftentimes excusing of a fault
Doth make the fault the worse by the excuse

À la chandelle, la chèvre semble demoiselle

By candlelight the nanny goat appears a maiden

Never choose your women or linen by candlelight

Il faut de tout pour faire un monde

You need a bit of everything to make a world

It takes all sorts to make a world

On ne change pas une équipe qui gagne

One doesn't change a winning team

Leave well alone

American *If it ain't broke, don't fix it*

Il a le bras long

He has a long arm

He has a finger in every pie

Quand le chat n'est pas là, les souris dansent

When the cat's away, the mice dance

When the cat's away, the mice will play

Chercher midi à quatorze heures

To look for midday at 2 o'clock

To split hairs

Medieval theology: *to count how many angels can dance on the head of a pin*

Qui prête aux amis perd au double

He who lends to friends loses twice

Shakespeare, Hamlet
Neither a borrower nor a lender be
For loan oft loses both itself and friend

La dernière goutte est celle qui fait déborder le vase

It is the last drop that makes the vase overflow

The last straw breaks the camel's back

On ne peut pas avoir le beurre et l'argent du beurre

You can't have both the butter and the money for butter

You can't both have your cake and eat it

Un bouillon de choux fait perdre au médecin cinq sous

A cabbage soup loses the doctor five sous

An apple a day keeps the doctor away

Ménager la chèvre et le chou

To handle the goat and the cabbage

To play both ends against the middle

Aujourd'hui en chair, demain en bière

Today in the flesh tomorrow in the coffin

Here today gone tomorrow

Les carottes sont cuites

[*Les carottes sont cuites* often used as a coded BBC radio message to the French Resistance in WWll]

The carrots are cooked

It is done and dusted

Jeter son froc aux orties

To throw one's habit in the nettles

To kick over the traces

Entre l'arbre et l'écorce, il ne faut pas mettre le doigt

Don't poke your finger between the bark and the tree

Curiosity killed the cat

Arabic proverb *Don't get between the onion and its skin*

Celui qui paye les violons choisit la musique

The one who pays the violinists chooses the music

He who pays the piper calls the tune

Il ne faut pas réveiller le chat qui dort

One must not waken the sleeping cat

Let sleeping dogs lie

C'est bonnet blanc et blanc bonnet

It's white hat and hat white

It's six of one and half a dozen of the other

L'économie de bouts de chandelle

Saving candle ends

To live on a shoe string

Il n'a pas inventé la poudre

He didn't invent gunpowder

He won't set the Thames on fire

Pas d'argent, pas de Suisses

No money, no Swiss [mercenaries]

No silver no servant

Entre le marteau et l'enclume

Between the hammer and the anvil

Between a rock and a hard place

Ted Kohler and Harold Arlen *Between the devil and the deep blue sea*

Chat échaudé craint l'eau froide

A scalded cat fears cold water

Once bitten, twice shy

Filer à l'anglaise

To steal away, English style

To take French leave

C'est une autre paire de manches

It's another pair of sleeves

It's another kettle of fish

Ça coûte les yeux de la tête

It costs the eyes of the head

It costs an arm and a leg

Revenons à nos moutons

[*French proverb often used untranslated*]

Let's return to our sheep

To get back to the nitty gritty

Une hirondelle ne fait pas le printemps

One swallow does not make spring

One swallow does not make a summer

Reculer pour mieux sauter

[*French proverb often used untranslated*]

To go back, the better to leap forward

One step back two steps forward

Construire des châteaux en Espagne

To build castles in Spain

To build castles in the air

Le flambeau de l'amour s'allume à la cuisine

The flame of love is kindled in the kitchen

The way to a man's heart is through his stomach

Il ne faut pas déshabiller Pierre pour habiller Paul

Don't undress Peter to dress Paul

Don't rob Peter to pay Paul

Bien bas choit qui trop monte

They fall far who climb too much

The higher they climb, the harder they fall

Le ventre ennoblit

The belly enobles

Shakespeare, Julius Caesar

Let me have men about me that are fat . . .
Yon Cassius has a lean and hungry look

C'est la paille et la poutre

It's the straw and the beam

It is the pot calling the kettle black

Si jeunesse savait, si vieillesse pouvait

If youth knew, if age could

George Bernard Shaw *Youth is wasted on the young*

Quand on avale le bœuf, il ne faut pas s'arrêter à la queue

When you swallow an ox you must not stop at the tail

Never do things by halves

Se lever du pied gauche

To get up on the left foot

To get out of bed on the wrong side

Heureux au jeu malheureux en amour

Lucky at cards unlucky in love

Dean Swift *Well, miss, you will have a sad husband, you have such good luck at cards*

Cherchez la femme

[French phrase used mainly by English speakers]

Look for the woman [as the cause]

Rudyard Kipling *The female of the species is more deadly than the male*

Se mélanger les pinceaux

To muddle one's paint brushes

To be at sixes and sevens

Avoir les yeux plus grand que l'estomac

To have eyes larger than one's stomach

To bite off more than you can chew

Il ne faut pas courir deux lièvres à la fois

One must not chase two hares at once

If you run after two hares, you will catch neither

Ça ferait rire les pierres

That would make stones laugh

It would make a cat laugh

Tel père, tel fils

Like father, like son

A chip off the old block